AGING WITH HEART

12 Inspiring Ways Women Over 50 Can Recover from Divorce, Betrayal, and Loss

A Free BONUS RESOURCE for you

www.FreeGiftFromRosemary.com

One in-depth training video on keeping your heart open through grief and betrayal

Rosemary O'Connor McKittrick, MA

WHAT OTHERS ARE SAYING ABOUT ROSEMARY O'CONNOR MCKITTRICK AND HER STRATEGIES

From grief to gratitude, Rosemary offers us a road map and a tool box for healing from loss and then navigating the terrain of major life change. Drawn from her own experience and the wisdom of many contemporary teachers, Rosemary brings real substance to our search for direction and purpose and a renewed sense of self with the gifts we have to bring the world after life falls apart. Insightful and empowering.

— WENDY SARNO, WRITER,
WRITINGSFROMWILDSOUL.COM, COLLECTED
ESSAYS AND POEMS

Thanks to Rosemary's sharing her personal journey, her wise observations and suggested pathways to recovery from loss, we're presented with opportunities to live experientially rather than intellectually.

— DORI SMITH, MA, ART HISTORIAN

I LOVE it!!!!!! It provides an alluring blueprint for a path to living fully in gratitude. Nicely done.

— GARY MCGRAIME, RETIRED OWNER, MCGRAIME
INTERIORS

We have all known someone that's stuck in a mindset of just following a path of accepting the unacceptable. Do you see change in yourself as walking into an abyss? Afraid you'll just free fall if you choose to be alone? Rosemary brings safety nets. You can overcome this. You can face your perceived fears, as she did. Explore how Rosemary saw being alone as an opportunity to find a life of rejuvenation, to overcome catastrophic thinking, and make changes to move on to a better life.

— WENDY TAYLOR, ARTIST

Rosemary came into my life like a breath of fresh air, sweeping away the doldrums I was stuck in regarding my own creative work. She generously shared her contagious enthusiasm, her strategies and sources, empowering me to get moving again in positive directions in all aspects of my life. Rosemary possesses that rare combination of true humility and daring courage it takes to look truth in the eye. Her work, her presence, and her example have been an invaluable gift.

— UMA MARKUS, MA, ART EDUCATOR AND
THERAPIST

This is a guide to a journey. Your journey. Take heart, it will have rewards you never dreamt possible

— PAIGE WEBSTER, *HAPPIER OLDER WOMAN*

The strategies in this book are invaluable for anyone who has encountered grief and betrayal on the journey, and who has not? Rosemary shares wisdom gleaned from her experience, pairs it with inspiration from familiar and well-loved authors, and the result ... a warm, positive, and practical guide for those who seek a return to happiness and fulfillment.

— MARTHA KARIPIN, MUSIC AND YOGA TEACHER

Rosemary O'Connor McKittrick captures the pain and guides you through the suffering to pure joy. It's a pleasure to join with her in this life journey.

— COLLEEN YOUNG, RETIRED PEACE CORPS

Rosemary carefully outlines a pathway to balanced, healthy self-care that is the basis for ultimate recovery. It's very difficult to fix a tool with the tool that's part of the problem. Rosemary emphasizes action. Her perspective is valuable

— T. N. TAYLOR, *PILGRIM ON LIFE'S ROAD*

TO LEARN ABOUT ROSEMARY'S BUSINESS CONSULTING, CONTACT HER AT:

RosemaryMcKittrick@comcast.net

MOTIVATE OTHERS!

"Share This Book"

Retail $17.95
Special quantity discounts

5-20 books	$16.95
21-99 books	$14.95
100-499 books	$12.95
500-999 books	$10.95
1000+ books	$9.95

To place an order, contact:
Rosemary O'Connor McKittrick
40 Calle Debra, Santa Fe, NM 87507
505-690-1841
RosemaryMcKittrick@comcast.net

PROFESSIONAL SPEAKER!

"For Your Next Event"

TO CONTACT OR BOOK
ROSEMARY O'CONNOR MCKITTRICK
TO SPEAK:

Rosemary O'Connor McKittrick
40 Calle Debra
Santa Fe, NM 87507
505-690-1841
RosemaryMcKittrick@comcast.net

COACHING FOR YOU!

If you're ready to overcome challenges and have major breakthroughs, you'll appreciate having Rosemary O'Connor McKittrick as your coach!

TO CONTACT:
Rosemary O'Connor McKittrick
40 Calle Debra
Santa Fe, NM 87507
505-690-1841
RosemaryMcKittrick@comcast.net

This book is dedicated to Jordan O'Connor McKittrick.
You've picked me up, dusted me off, and sent me back out
to the playing field more times than I can remember. To be
loved the way you love me is a gift.

Thank you,
Mama

CONTENTS

A MESSAGE TO YOU!

Sometimes it takes a heartbreak to shake us awake and help us see we are worth so much more than we're settling for. —Mandy Hale, American writer

Have you had times in your life when you hit rough patches? About ten years ago, my life took an unexpected turn. I was married 35 years. Like any couple, we both made plenty of mistakes along the way and had our share of breakdowns and breakthroughs. We always managed to work things out and find our way back to each other. What I knew for certain was—we were a team. We were committed to each other and our marriage.

I was wrong.

On the drive back home from a baby shower one winter afternoon, my husband explained to me he was living a double life. Hearing about his lifetime of betrayal dumbfounded me. I was all in. He had been the moral authority in our home. I realized somewhere between carpooling kids, managing work deadlines, grocery shopping, and getting dinner on the table, I missed the red flags. I was spinning inside a web of secrets for over three decades, and I was speaking with a person I had not met before.

It was hard to walk away from a marriage I thought was real. It was harder to forgive myself for being blind. If we live in a culture of narcissism, as some historians say we do, then I got a dose of narcissistic traits in my marriage.

In one way, I realized I could only feel heartache like this over someone I loved so dearly. I also watched as the trust and sense of safety I had known in the relationship dissolved. I realized you can't have a *real* relationship with someone who's wearing a mask.

It's an age-old story. I just didn't realize it was our story, and he was off vacationing with the next true love.

How do I explain this to our kids? To the family? I know life is messy, but this was something else. *Integrity is how you behave when no one is watching,* wrote C. S. Lewis, British author. And some people, I discovered, you learn to love from a distance.

Learning about people who lead double lives (mostly men) and embracing the pain and powerlessness that I felt was the beginning of my healing journey. Treating myself with the utmost tenderness turned out to be the *best* medicine. I realized I needed to learn to take care of myself before I could really care for anyone else. Confidence today is knowing I have my own back and I can handle what comes my way.

Someone I loved once gave me a box full of darkness. It took me years to understand that this too, was a gift, wrote Mary Oliver, American poet.

There wasn't one *aha* moment when I woke up from my trance to a larger reality. Once the tornado in my head cleared a little, I heard a faint voice from inside. *Time to get moving.*

That was the beginning.

Grief is love with no place to go, said Jamie Anderson, English author.

We're taught how to acquire things in life, not what to do when we lose them. You already know grief isn't for sissies. I want to share with you strategies I've found valuable on my journey. This book is a blueprint, of sorts, for stepping out of your trance and back into your life.

Are you game? There's only one requirement. You're responsible for your own comeback. Taking responsibility means you no longer blame outside circumstances, other people, or past events for the conditions of your life. Fear is something we all experience. Courage is doing what you're afraid of doing anyway, and that's what this book is about. You may think you're *too old* and *too set* in your ways to make changes. You're not. Change your mind. That's the start. The belief that you're *too old* doesn't serve the person you are.

This book is a toolkit for getting back on your feet and letting go of outdated strategies. It's about action, not thinking.

You may discover grief and betrayal can be powerful teachers. For you, it might be the death of a loved one, a beloved pet, job loss, breakup of a romantic relationship, retirement, legal issues, or divorce. It doesn't matter. Grief is grief, and loss is loss. The words here speak to your journey.

Owning your story and loving yourself through the whole sacred catastrophe is the most courageous thing you can do for yourself. It gives you power to rewrite your ending, live true to your own values, and stand up for what matters with integrity and a wise and caring heart.

I invite you to read this book not so much from a space of learning something new, but more from a space of remembering. There's an innate wisdom in you that already knows this stuff. Unfortunately, some of us have built-in forgetters.

This is your nudge to remember, one tool in your arsenal of recovery. It's not a replacement for working with a skilled grief or trauma therapist. You may need that. Whatever it takes.

There are tools here that can make a difference in your life. Some may seem overly simple. The simple things helped me most, like remembering to pause and take a deep breath before opening my mouth and putting my foot in it. You're grieving, no question! All kinds of feelings, from anger to despair, are floating around in the mix. Do you really want to dump unwarranted negativity on the people around you? Pausing gives you space. Otherwise, the first comment out of your mouth is usually emotional and probably something you'll regret saying later. The ego speaks first and loudest. Pausing allows you to respond appropriately and not react foolishly. What you put out is what you get back, and you don't need to manufacture more misery for yourself.

You'll hear about staying connected to people. Isolation is a mistake when you're grieving. You'll hear about ways to build your energy and maintain a commitment to your goals. One of the most important pieces in this process is having a *go for*—some goal that's bigger than you are—maybe something you care about more than yourself. Dream a new dream for yourself! It will keep you moving ahead when roadblocks seem insurmountable. Life coach Tony Robbins calls this creating a compelling future. Getting clear on *why* your goal is a must is critical. Strategies will follow. Your limiting beliefs will try to stop you. In reality, the only thing holding you back is your belief that you can't come back from this.

Finding ways to calm your roving, runaway mind is essential. Energy is everything in this process, and when you beat yourself up, your energy goes down. Without energy, there's no change. In this book, you'll uncover ways of paying attention to how you *be* in the world and what needs tweaking. You'll hear about taking uncomfortable action and catching worry and morbid reflection as it rears its ugly head. Worry, someone said, is like a rocking chair. It keeps you moving, but you're going nowhere.

Relax. Show up. Let yourself be seen and remember laughter. It helps with adrenalized anxiety. You can't always fix problems, but sometimes you can see the funniness in them.

Hold yourself in kindness and tend to your heart instead of your hurt. When you come from your heart, no one can stop you. As you make your way through the abyss of your own grief, loss, or betrayal, know you have lots of company on the road, no matter how old you are.

I honor your courage, and at 74, I'm on the road with you. Progress. Not perfection. Keep opening.

Take off your armor, dare to be vulnerable, dare to unwrap yourself, and dare yourself to be yourself, said Maria Shriver, American journalist.

MANIFESTO OF THE BRAVE AND BROKENHEARTED

There is no greater threat to the critics and cynics and fear mongers than those of us who are willing to fall because we have learned to rise.

With skinned knees and bruised hearts; we choose owning our stories of struggle, over hiding, over hustling, over pretending.

When we deny our stories, they define us. When we run from struggle, we are never free. So we turn toward truth and look it in the eye.

We will not be characters in our stories. Not villains, not victims, not even heroes.

We are the authors of our lives. We write our own daring endings.

We craft love from heartbreak, compassion from shame, grace from disappointment, courage from failure. Showing up is our power. Story is our way home. Truth is our song. We are the brave and brokenhearted. We are rising strong.

—Brené Brown, *Rising Strong*

Chapter 1

Grief Has Its Own Time

You will lose someone you can't live without, and your heart will be badly broken, and the bad news is that you never completely get over the loss of your beloved. But this is also the good news. They live forever in your broken heart that doesn't seal back up. And you come through. It's like having a broken leg that never heals perfectly—that still hurts when the weather gets cold, but you learn to dance with the limp. —Anne Lamott

When we grieve, we allow ourselves to feel the truth of our pain, the measure of betrayal or tragedy in our life. By our willingness to mourn, we slowly acknowledge, integrate, and accept the truth of our losses. Sometimes, the best way to let go is to simply grieve.

—Jack Kornfield, American writer and teacher

GRIEF IS ABOUT A BROKEN HEART, not a broken brain, and acute grief can stun the heart. In the brain, grief shows up as a threat to survival. You probably heard the phrase *broken heart* syndrome. Physicians don't fully understand the syndrome or its basic causes. It's usually temporary, with symptoms lasting a few days to a few weeks. Chest pain and shortness of breath are some of the symptoms.

The important point is that grief lives in your mind and your body, and both need tender loving care. Mentally working through traumatic events and settling your frazzled nervous system is the way home. Tending to both is the elixir. The two can meet, recalibrate, and integrate. You *can* handle this.

Grief is a rite of passage. Speaking to groups, I stress this.

A fearless, compassionate softness toward your pain is called for here. You've been through a lot and you're stepping into unchartered territory. Gentleness allows you to stand honestly in what happened. Find someone who will also witness your pain, someone to simply listen to you and get what's true for you.

Breathe. Slow down. Take it easy. Gentleness breeds courage.

———

The reality is that you'll grieve forever. You'll not 'get over' the loss of a loved one; you'll learn to live with it. You'll heal and you'll rebuild yourself around the loss you've suffered. You'll be whole again, but you'll never be the same. Nor should you be the same, nor would you want to.
—Elisabeth Kübler-Ross, Swiss-American psychiatrist

When you watch yourself going into emotional or mental overload, see if you can catch that experience as it arises and

PAUSE. Take a few deep breaths and keep breathing. Conscious breathing stimulates the lymphatic system, meaning it detoxifies your body. It also lowers your blood pressure, calms you down, and increases your energy levels. This sounds simple, but it works. Set your best intention for what you want to see happen in the situation confronting you. Intention steers everything; it sets the compass of your heart.

The tough part is remembering to notice the changes in your breathing when you first start getting stressed out. Your breath gets shallow. Deepen it.

Rebooting your life takes trying new behaviors and seeing what works and doesn't. This is about you taking your life into your own hands. There's no one-size fits all here. What's important is that you stay open and remain coachable. Whatever is blocked within you nurtures fear. Fear blocks your energy. Breathe.

Acupuncture can help. Long-term studies show that acupuncture helps to ground the body; it's a physical and emotional re-balancing of your energy system. You may sleep better. Acupuncture helps with headaches, chemotherapy-induced and postoperative nausea, vomiting, fibromyalgia, osteoarthritis, and it can also lower back pain.

The Dalai Lama was getting ready to teach about happiness. Someone asked him how he could teach on happiness given the Chinese had destroyed 5,000 of his temples and monasteries, stamped out Tibetan religious traditions, and tortured and murdered more than a million of his people. To many, it seemed like an inconceivable task. The Dalai Lama agreed it was true. They had destroyed his temples and monasteries, stamped out Tibetan religious traditions, and tortured and murdered his people.

But he also said he wasn't willing for the Chinese to steal his happiness as well. He had no control over their behavior. The only thing he could control was his response to their behavior. His happiness was his, and he wasn't giving that up for the Chinese.

You can't make others feel what is right and wrong, he said. *You can't teach them integrity. You also can't allow them to go that deep into your mind and heart to where they can hurt you.* You can only control yourself, and that's where your attention belongs. That's where the power is. *Your prime purpose,* he added, *is to live in the world and help others, and if you can't help others, at least don't hurt them.*

In his own life, the Dalai Lama lost his beloved tutor, his mother, father, and his brother. Grief and anxiety came naturally to him. But he cautioned against allowing the experience of loss to continue on and on. Left unchecked, he said it leads to a kind of self-absorption, a feeling like you're the only one who experiences loss. Reality reminds you that loss is a natural part of life. It happens to all of us. We're all in the same boat. It's part of our common humanity. In that sense, you're never isolated in your sorrow, even though, it may look and feel that way in the moment.

Self-compassion plays a big role in tending to grief. It's about offering the same kindness to yourself you would offer to a child. This way of thinking allows you to respond to heartache with understanding rather than blame and shame.

Imperfections are part of being human. In a study of people whose marriages fell apart, what made the biggest difference in people moving on after divorce wasn't how long their marriages lasted or the things they did to bounce back. What made the biggest difference was self-compassion. Blaming your behavior on your mistakes rather than your character allows you to feel guilt instead of shame.

The distinction between the two is important. Guilt is about, *I did a bad thing*. Shame is about, *I'm a bad person*. Guilt keeps you moving forward. Shame makes you feel small and worthless. Writing is a great tool for cultivating self-compassion and processing trauma hurts. Get the words out. Put them down on paper. It'll help you work through your anxiety and upset.

Chapter 2

Courage Isn't Always Loud

Life becomes easier when you learn to accept an apology you never got.

—Robert Brault

You have to open yourself up and let the pain move through you ... It's not yours to hold. —Frank Ostaseski, Founding Director, Zen Hospice Project

YOU CAN ONLY PULL the covers up over your head for so long. At some point, you got to get up, get on, or give up. These are your choices.

None of what I'm saying matters if you don't take action. You're redesigning your internal and external landscape. The deconstruction process is building your clarity on a deeper level. It's going to feel weird at first. You're shifting decades of old conditioning. That's good news!

Life is about curve balls. The question is, what will you do in the face of loss? Who are you going to be? I've seen the strategies I'm talking about work with people I consult.

As suggested, journal and record your thoughts. Sense your longings. Nothing changes until you bring your experience into awareness in the present. Journaling makes it concrete. Here are a few questions to ask yourself. What's your current agreement with life? Does your current agreement need updating? What's your heart's deepest intention? What is it you must accomplish before you die?

Now move from your thoughts to your feelings about what you journaled. How do you feel? Can you locate in your body where these feelings live? What's the experience? Tight? Burning? Be curious, not judgmental. You're being a sleuth, studying your patterns, collecting information, and learning what triggers you and where in your body it shows up or not. Sometimes triggers aren't conscious and they're nothing to avoid. Triggers are signs that something needs to be attended to and integrated.

Softening to your experience and allowing it to be here is everything. Knowledge is power. Is your jaw tight? Your breath shallow? Your belly hard? Breathe into these tight areas and soften the hardness through conscious breathing. You're letting go of a grief-holding pattern you probably developed over a lifetime.

As the experience of grief in your mind and body is met with softness instead of contempt, you'll begin to relax. The mind part of your experience responds with kindness, a kindness that may be new to you. You start filling the space once occupied with contempt for your pain into kindness. It's not about loving your pain. It's about sending love to yourself even though you're in pain. If you take action, you'll open the door to your future. If not now, when? If not you, who?

When I loved myself enough, I began leaving whatever wasn't healthy. This meant people, jobs, my own beliefs and habits—anything that kept me small. My judgment called it disloyal. Now I see it as self-loving.
—Kim McMillen, American author

Healing and moving on are about learning to acknowledge and allow space for your grief to show itself. Grief doesn't have an expiration date, and like love, can be limitless. Don't lie to yourself or others about your pain, either. There's nothing wrong with you because you're having so many feelings. You're making peace with your sorrow. Be willing to forgive yourself for the mistakes you made along the way, and be grateful for the lessons learned.

Grief takes what it takes. Your job is to allow it. Getting back in the game can sometimes be the hardest part. No one can really tell you how to handle your grief. Your grief is yours. As you know, it's not just about tears and anguish. Grief can be about recalling the laughter and great times you shared, too. The earlier you allow yourself to begin grieving, the better. In truth, it's what you need most right now. Approach it in whatever way feels right to you, and don't punish yourself because you got left behind in life. Don't punish yourself if you fall apart in public, months, or years later. It's okay. When you love and lose someone, you grieve. The possibility is that the death or departure can one day spark a new life for you. You can learn to live a full life again, even with a hole in your heart. It takes time. Our society doesn't give much weight to acknowledging and tending to grief. The job is yours.

Self-compassion is the medicine you need as you get more comfortable with your uncomfortableness. Human beings are wired for struggle. It's part of the human condition. The way out of struggle is through it. Your willingness to name the hurt, and feel the hurt, rather than bury it, means everything. If you reflect on life, it's often through the tough times you learned the most. Bring your attention back to the present moment as much as possible. All points of power exist in the moment. When you notice yourself straying into the past or future, gently bring your attention back to the moment. You're flexing a new muscle. Treat yourself like you already are the person you want to be. You're seeing the mystery of life in action as opposed to the way you had it all wired up. Keep offering gestures of kindness to yourself and ground yourself in the moment.

You're where you are in life because of the choices you made. Let today be the day you stop being haunted by the past because there's no power in victimhood.

I eventually came to understand that in harboring the anger, the bitterness and resentment towards those that had hurt me, I was giving the reins of control over to them. Forgiving was not about accepting their words and deeds. Forgiving was about letting go and moving on with my life. —Isabel Lopez, American editor

Chapter 3

Get Fired Up

To embark on the journey towards your goals and dreams requires bravery. To remain on that path requires courage. The bridge that merges the two is commitment. —Steve Maraboli

Action is a great restorer and builder of confidence. Inaction is not only the result, but the cause of fear. Perhaps the action you take will be successful; perhaps different action or adjustments will have to follow. But any action is better than no action at all. —Norman Vincent Peale, American clergyman

YOU GET WHAT YOU'RE committed to. Self-defeating mindsets stop you.

I work with people to move beyond the mindset of I'm too old, too fat, too set in my ways, too hard of hearing, too exhausted, too whatever, to change. I'll have another piece of cake, thank you!

You're remodeling your life first and foremost. You're freeing yourself of outdated beliefs, many of which you adopted as a kid or accepted from people who were not very successful in their own lives. As an adult, an update is probably overdue.

This book is about you stepping up for you.

Aging with an open heart, as mentioned, is about self-care foremost, which many of us flunked while we were running around, ensuring everyone's drink glass was full. In our culture, women tend to put themselves last. It's like we were bred to be domestics. Everyone else's needs were more immediate and more important. Burnout and exhaustion thrive in this climate.

Self-care is any physical, emotional, or mental thing you consciously do to take care of yourself. It's not self-indulgence. It's self-preservation.

Look at your commitments. Start saying no to things you don't necessarily have to do, things that take up too much of your time and energy, things you're not committed to. If you're loyal to people and projects that don't fit with your values anymore, decide which ones go and which ones stay. This is also a good exercise in boundary setting.

Schedule time for things that bring you joy and help you relax, like loafing, long walks, hiking, steamy baths, reading, and hanging with friends. Pay attention to your self-talk, too.

Reach out and ask for help when you need it. Whether you need a hand setting up your backyard drip system or you're just in need of a kind ear to listen to what happened today at work, pick up the phone and call someone. You can break up negative self-talk by simply reaching out and accepting a helping hand.

Jennie Owens was burned out taking care of her three small kids. She was unable to greet them in a loving way when they bolted through the door each day after day-camp. She was so stressed out she wasn't able to give them much of anything at all. Something needed to change. The kids had one more week left at camp before being home full-time with Jennie and requiring mom to give even more. Jennie needed help. She decided to make the most of her final week at home by herself. This was going to be Jennie's week. With the kids at camp and her husband at work, she met up with friends at a local coffee shop. She took long walks. She read for pure pleasure. She even scheduled a massage for herself. Anything Jennie could think of that was purely for Jennie, she did. She also learned a valuable lesson about kicking back. At the end of her self-imposed retreat, Jennie's husband commented.

What happened to you, he asked? A week earlier Jennie was biting off everyone's head who looked or spoke to her in the wrong way. Not only was she mean to her family, she was causing problems for other people around her.

After only a week of self-pampering, Jennie began to relax. She was able to meet the kids at the door with a sincere kiss and a smile. She was able to be the wife and mom she was committed to being. She was no Mother Teresa. But she was moving in the direction of positive change. Just one-day-at-a-time made it doable.

Stay present. You can't change what you're unaware of. And it's okay to start with baby steps. It's your turn now. It doesn't have to be big stuff, just things that give you pleasure, like a bouquet of fresh flowers on your breakfast table. A gift from you to you.

Spend at least a half-hour a day outdoors. Take off your socks and shoes and walk in the grass or dirt for 20 minutes. Remember to drink lots of water. That pot of chili you've been thinking about, go ahead, make it for yourself. Don't wait for company. Do it for you. What about your back pain? You've been promising yourself a visit to the chiropractor for months. Sleep, diet, and exercise really matter.

Movement is everything. Find something physical like walking, yoga, Zumba, anything that gets your heart rate going, and do it regularly. You'll see a shift. Yoga is a coming home to your body. It quiets your over-active mind and teaches you to listen to your body. With yoga, you become aware of how and where you're restricted. It's a powerful teacher.

Pay attention to what supports you and do more of that. If you have to, paste sticky notes up on the frig to remind yourself about your new regime. All progress comes from breaking old patterns. Don't let fear stop you.

Take a break. Studies show that when you take breaks, you're more productive. Keep thinking about special things to do for yourself. Something as simple as sinking into those fresh sheets you just put on your bed can feel delicious. Ultimately, there's no one out there you can fix, manage, or save, but yourself, so start nurturing you. You're your most important relationship, and when you stop running on empty, you have more to offer everybody. You end up teaching others how to love you by how you love yourself.

Chapter 4

What If You Can?

It is not in the stars to hold our destiny but in ourselves. —William Shakespeare

The only thing I know for sure (after all the research I have done on courage, shame and vulnerability) is that if you are going to dare greatly, you're going to get your ass kicked at some point. If you choose courage, you will absolutely know failure, disappointment, setback, even heartbreak. That's why we call it courage. That's why it is so rare.

—Brené Brown, American author

YOU'RE A LOT BIGGER than what's on your plate right now.

Do you ever wonder why you decide to make changes in your life and nothing changes? Why is it that things don't stick?

It's about your belief system, what you decided was possible for yourself in life. A lot of these disempowering beliefs you inherited, and you're living out of them today. Beliefs are self-fulfilling prophecies. If you have a core belief of—*I don't really have what it takes in life to finish anything*—then where do you think it leads? Look around. I suspect you'll see all the unfinished business of your life around you.

Your identity is the sum total of all the beliefs. Your identity is your current comfort zone in life. It's where you're willing to go to … and then stop. Are you living with an obsolete operating system? Speaking to groups, I would take a deeper cut on this point. Identity controls everything: what you perceive, how you feel, think, interact with people, and what you are willing to do and not do. Identity is the control system in the human personality. It's the lens through which you view life.

Humans naturally stay consistent with how they define themselves. It's like you built a small box, jumped inside, and closed the lid over your head. You can't breathe or move inside, but you forgot you're the one who built the box, jumped inside, and closed the lid. As long as you continue to tell yourself the same old stories about how limited you are, the stories continue to be true.

Change your story and you'll change your life.

Dr. Maya Angelou grew up hearing phrases like *dream big* and *nothing is impossible*. The words didn't fit the world she lived in. She was raped at age seven by her mother's boyfriend. For the next five years, she was mute. She dropped out of high school and returned to school as a pregnant teenager. She worked as a streetcar conductor, waitress, and a madam for prostitutes. By most people's standards, her life was bleak.

Despite her history, Maya went on to become one of the most influential writers in America. She spoke six languages, received more than 30 honorary degrees, and was the second poet in history to share one of her poems at a presidential inauguration. Maya started with nothing, a classic rags to riches story.

I have great respect for the past, Maya said. *If you don't know where you've come from, you don't know where you're going. I have respect for the past, but I'm a person of the moment. I'm here, and I do my best to be completely centered at the place I'm at, then I go forward to the next place.*

Maya unpacked her life in an extraordinary way. Her invitation is not to ignore your past, but to focus on living in the now. Raise your standards. Be willing to expand your sense of what's possible.

If you raise your standards but don't really believe you can meet them, you've already sabotaged yourself. You won't even try; you'll lack the sense of certainty that allows you to tap the deepest capacity that's within yourself ... Our beliefs are like unquestioned commands, telling us how things are, what's possible and impossible and what we can and cannot do. They shape every action, every thought, and every feeling that we experience. As a result, changing our belief systems is central to making any real and lasting change in our lives. —Tony Robbins, American life-coach

Resilience comes from deep inside you and from those who stand by you. People recover more quickly when they realize their hardships aren't entirely their fault and that these hardships won't last forever or follow them around forever. Not everything that happens to you happens because of you. Taking things personally is a slippery slope, and blaming yourself stalls recovery.

For most people who live with grief, they say that over time, sadness gets better. Humans are wired for connection and grief, and you also have the tools to recover from both. Heartbreak is part of life. None of us escapes. In that sense, you're connected to something much larger than you. These losses are your defining moments, your wake-up calls. Your time is running out. How you deal with loss going forward affects everything. Whoever you thought you were before, you're now someone else. You're creating a new identity.

What you believe to be true about what happened opens or closes you to new possibilities. You shape your brain based on your repeated thoughts, and what you practice grows stronger. It takes awareness to catch yourself ruminating about the past or dreading the future, and to gently coax your attention back to the moment.

Can you see how certain thoughts and beliefs limit you? You can change limiting beliefs. You don't have to get stuck in heartbreak. No matter what the culture or love songs say, true fulfillment doesn't come from the outside. It's an inside job. Waiting to be completed by that special someone is a myth. You were born complete. Fulfillment is something you bring to the party, not something you search for at the party.

Chapter 5

Flying Solo

I used to think that the worst thing in life was to end up all alone. It's not. The worst thing in life is ending up with people who make you feel all alone.
–Robin Williams

Use loneliness. Its ache creates urgency to reconnect with the world. Take that aching and use it to propel you deeper into your need for expression —to speak, to say who you are. —Natalie Goldberg, American author

YOU'RE LOOKING IN THE MIRROR and realizing you never expected to be alone.

There has been a radical shift in our society in the last fifty years. One out of seven people lives alone today, and three out of five people report feeling lonesome and disconnected. This is especially true for women because women typically outlive men. High blood pressure, depression, heart disease, and stroke have all been associated with loneliness.

We're social animals, and we depend on each other for survival. The desire for a relationship is a biologically rooted state that motivates you to reach out. Recent research reveals that loneliness correlates higher with early death than does obesity and smoking a pack of cigarettes a day. From an evolutionary point of view, loneliness also has a positive purpose—to nudge you to connect. Your connections play a huge part in how you think, what you do, and how you see yourself. Don't isolate. Reach out.

Loneliness also correlates with high media use. It's good to stay up-to-date with what's happening in the world, but enough already. The nightly news drowns you in merciless news because bad news sells. Authentically connecting to another human being heals loneliness, not the media. Turn off your TV. At least for a bit. You can't really fill the empty places in your life with TV. It just looks that way. Know when to cut yourself a break and when to engage or disengage from the online world.

Not everyone who lives alone is lonely. I'm not speaking about solitude here, which can be rich and revitalizing. I'm talking about the ache that comes when you feel something is really wrong and you're hurting.

The global pandemic deepened the experience of loneliness for many. Others appreciated the solitude and convenience Zoom brought to their lives. It's not about what's happening in your life. It's about how you hold what's happening. That's the key. By letting go, you create space in your life. You're learning how to walk with grief in a new way. Remember to reach out.

How do you free yourself? In the deepest sense, you free yourself by finding yourself, simply permit the pain to come into your heart and pass through. If you do that, it will pass. —Michael Singer, American author

Grief begs you to open your heart. It asks you to bring loving kindness to the places that hurt the most, like your heart. These are the places in the past you turned away from in fear, judgment, and distrust. The dark night of the soul lives here. You're attending to unattended sorrow. The refusal to own your pain turns it into suffering.

Can you accept the unacceptable? If you can open up even a little bit, surrender will start to free you. None of us escapes grief. Your relationship with your beloved is not over, it simply changed.

There's an intuitive process called *heart speech*. It's a way to send blessings directly from your heart to the people you lost. You visualize the person in your mind and silently wish them well on their journey. You say goodbye while maintaining a heart connection. Keep talking to them and don't be surprised if you hear an answer. You're integrating your grief with love and concern for their well-being. It helps to clear the path for you, and who knows, it may help the departed get complete with you as well. You're speaking heart to heart.

Unattended sorrow is stored in the mind and body. The point is to breathe and soften, soften your muscles, your flesh, and your bones. Go to the edge of where it hurts most, breathe and soften. You may experience grief you've been holding onto for a lifetime. What is this pain about? What needs to be expressed? What does the pain need?

The mental counterpart to softening your body is mercy. You're bringing kindness and mercy to the places within you that you sidestepped before. Mercy often shows up as forgiveness for yourself or others. The last stage of working with mental and physical sorrow is making peace with sorrow. Forgive and be thankful for the tough lessons learned that brought you to this place of letting go. When you meet fear and grief with kindness, the energy you've been using to hold back releases.

You may have been running away from pain for so long, you sometimes forget how to deal with it. When you allow your heart and mind to stay open to the process, you begin to experience relief and are less activated when it revisits you. It isn't sadness that limits your access to the heart, it's your wish for it to be some other way. Where are you going? In the wrong direction? What needs to shift here? Pause when you're agitated or doubtful, take a step back, breathe, and rethink the situation.

I would speak with groups about clearing away the muck, reaching out for help, and finding the best version of themselves through community with others.

The only safety lies in letting it all in—the wild and the weak; fear, fantasies, failures and success. When loss rips off the doors of the heart, or sadness veils your vision with despair, practice becomes simply bearing the truth. In the choice to let go of your known way of being, the whole world is revealed to your new eyes. —Danna Faulds, American poet

Chapter 6

There's A Whole World Waiting

Make your vision so clear that your fears become irrelevant. —Anonymous

Our ability to connect with others is innate, wired into our nervous systems, and we need connection as much as we need physical nourishment. —Sharon Salzberg, American author

WHEN YOU EXPERIENCE GRIEF and loss, it's natural to want to curl up, lick your wounds, and isolate. Please don't. Healing happens in a community with people. It happens with those people and in those groups where you feel safe enough to share those deep hurts.

If you have family and close friends who love and listen to you, use them. If not, don't stop. Most communities offer bereavement and grief support groups. Find a skilled therapist if you need one.

Grief and betrayal can bring you to a breaking point, to a humbling where you experience powerlessness like you never have before. The path to recovery grows out of welcoming grief as your companion for now, as painful as it is, and being open to allowing it to move through you.

The cornerstone of coming back is you tending to you. You may not feel like taking the time to nurture yourself right now, but it's more important now than ever. Either tell someone your story or write out your story in your journal. These are two powerful ways to come to terms with loss. Each time you revisit what happened with another person or with your pen, it reduces the charge that pulls you back into the past and keeps you stuck. Pick the best listener you know and be respectful of their time because you may need to tell your story to them again. Telling your story in a safe environment helps to unfreeze your troubled brain. Recovering from grief and shattered trust takes time.

Playing your story over and over again in your mind paralyzes you. Argue for your misery, and it's yours. As much as possible, ground yourself in the moment, and bring your attention back to the present when you notice it straying. Singing, humming, chanting, a warm bath, gently rocking yourself—all of these can be calming. If your thoughts are too overwhelming right now, back off, take a walk or take a nap. Always err on the side of being patient and kind with yourself. If you're so inclined, try dancing, painting, sculpting, collages, or cooking. You're bringing your feelings into form and expressing them. You're learning to listen to yourself in the deepest way, developing courage of the heart. It's not like the physical courage of bungee jumping off bridges. It's the courage to take a deeper cut on your life, to investigate, see what's true, and to be open. Learning to be with things as they are can take time, and it's not about struggling, it's about opening. Take your life into your own hands!

Pay attention to all the little ways goodness already shows up in your life throughout the day. Notice simple things, like the smell and taste of that warm cup of tea in your hands, the blueness of this morning's sky, or the sweet smile of the clerk who waited on you at the grocery store. Goodness shows up when you open yourself up to seeing it.

If you have been touched by addiction in any way, know that 12-step groups save lives, and they address more than addiction. They offer a design for living, a place where you go and experience firsthand that you're not alone in your grief. Others may not share your exact story, but loss is loss. In 12-step, you realize your way of thinking is a big part of the problem. You also learn to live your way into a new way of thinking. You'll discover you don't have to keep manufacturing bogeymen in your life. You learn to face what needs to be faced with the tools and support you're receiving.

The Serenity Prayer

God grant me the serenity to accept the things
I cannot change, the courage to change the things
I can, and the wisdom to know the difference.

Powerful words! If you don't like the *God* word, replace it with the Universe, the Great Mystery, Nature, or whatever does it for you. It's God as *you* understand God. Getting clear on what you *can* and *can't* change can save a lifetime of suffering. No kidding! How does that saying go?

Maybe it's time to take the cotton out of your ears and put it in your mouth.

We believe it takes a strong back and a soft front to face the world.
—Joan Halifax, American Buddhist teacher

Challenges are inevitable in life, and it's never too late to start over. Demanding life should be problem free is delusion, and when you argue with reality, you lose. I address this issue regularly with the people I coach. Set the intention to start seeing the way things actually are instead of how you decided they should be. Your misconceptions about life are crushing you. Develop a new relationship with your problems. You can't change what happened, but you can always change your attitude about what happened. Don't build a big story around your mess. Drama amplifies the situation. You're developing courage of the heart. Try facing the moment without your story. Keep breathing and bringing yourself back to the present. Feel your feelings. See what happens.

From my experience, there's nothing more important to true growth than realizing you're not the voice of your mind. You're not your thoughts. You're not your feelings. You're not your story.

You're the one who hears all of it. You're the witness, the awareness of it all, and you're bringing the light of that awareness to your grief, loss, and fear. Slow down, be open to a new way of experiencing life. You can learn to live from your highest self.

We're all running out of time. You want to be as loving as possible going forward. Only have people in your life who share your values.

Chapter 7

Here Is Perfect

The critical ingredient is getting off your butt and doing something. It's as simple as that. A lot of people have ideas, but there are few people who decide to do anything about them now. —Nolan Bushnell

Blackbird singing in the dead of night
Take these broken wings and learn to fly
All your life
You were only waiting for this moment to arise
You were only waiting for this moment to arise
—The Beatles

YOU'RE NOT TOO OLD. Honest! That's the superstition you need to eliminate right now. If you want to really take off, you have to get beyond what's holding you down, and it's not about how old you are. It's about how you *view* how old you are. People I coach tell me shifting this mindset is key.

Just get started.

Make a point of reading something or listening to something every day that inspires you. This simple task takes you outside of your limiting beliefs about what's possible for you. It doesn't need to take long. Thirty minutes is good. Just pick something and do it daily. The car or gym are great places for audio. Your alternative is to sit and ruminate about your problems. You already know the rabbit hole that launches you down. Pop those earbuds in and get started. It's brainwashing that works. The key is consistency. Make it a part of your daily routine.

Whoever and whatever you thought you were before, you're something new now. You're birthing a new identity. So much of this process is learning to be comfortable with your uncomfortableness. It's called growth.

Your heart knows the answers to your deepest desires. Listen.

It doesn't matter if you're single, separated, divorced, or widowed. We live in a family-orientated culture, and there's a certain stigma about being single. An awkwardness might exist now among those you care about as everyone adjusts to your new identity, an identity that was once defined by marriage or partnership. A period of adjustment happens. Your single status may show up as threatening to some; for others, it may be a reminder of something they don't want to have to face. It's too close. It reminds them this could happen to them. The good news is you'll discover who your real friends are in the process.

Our culture offers up a belief that you'll be happy when something good happens to you on the outside or when some other person comes along and loves you. Music, advertising, storybooks, and films peddle this philosophy. As I said, it really is a myth. The truth is, you're already complete. Before anyone or anything got added to the mix, you were whole. You just forgot! Coming to an understanding of this is at the heart of the hero's journey.

Whatever you think you lost and whatever you think is missing plays an important role in healing what feels broken inside. If you understand who you *are*, you're better able to handle the heartbreak that comes your way. You're better able to stay calm in the midst of chaos. Life will show you all the places needing your attention, all the places you neglected. The hero's journey is about recovering and nurturing these parts and remembering who you are.

Anything new you take on feels awkward at first. Do it anyway. The way to break old habits is to replace them with new habits. It's about stepping out of your comfort zone. You *can* teach an old dog new tricks, if you say so!

Stuff happens. Hold what shows up in your life as a challenge, not a problem. You're about creating breakthroughs in your life now. A breakthrough is an opening in time when something new can happen, something clicks and you start seeing life in a new way. Develop that muscle. Stay solution orientated. Catch yourself doing things right instead of wrong and give yourself a pat on the back. Make decisions and follow through.

That's the goal.

Find yourself a role model. There's somebody out there who's already living the life you want. Look around and see who that is for you. Copy their behavior.

When I think of my version of a role model, it's not about being the perfect Samaritan; it's just being out there and being honest and happily imperfect. —Zoe Kravitz, American actress

Who do you go to when you're lost and need advice from someone? It might also be a world leader or an author you admire. Doesn't matter.

Role models teach you how to live with integrity, optimism, hope, and compassion. I'm thinking you can use some of that about now. They also remind you to be courageous and see the best in yourself.

You're viewing life with new eyes. What happened is over. It can't be undone. What you can do is use what happened to forgive yourself, forgive someone else, or simply decide to start over. You may need to step back from commitments for a bit so you can reconnect with yourself in an authentic way. What can you give to yourself that you're demanding from someone else? What support do you need from others you're not asking for? What are you believing that's causing you fear? What choices have you made that are limiting you? When you get quiet, it's easier to hear the answers to these questions.

Something ended or someone died, and you lost some of your innocence. Moving on in your life allows you to create your future. Isn't this why you're reading this book? Letting go is about releasing whatever binds you to the past. You're being called to step into a new life.

It may not be the life you imagined, but it's your life. You came here for a reason. Is it time for you to go and begin again? —Doug Cooper, American artist

Chapter 8

Your Carriage Awaits

A champion is someone who gets up, even when he can't. —Jack Dempsey

Until you are committed, there is hesitancy, the chance to draw back, always ineffectiveness. Concerning all acts of initiative (and creation), there is one elementary truth, the ignorance of which kills countless ideas and splendid plans: That the moment one definitely commits oneself, then Providence moves, too. All sorts of things occur to help one that would never otherwise have occurred. A whole stream of events issues from the decision, raising in one's favor all manner of unforeseen incidents and meetings and material assistance, which no man could have dreamt would have come his way. I have learned a deep respect for one of Goethe's couplets. Whatever you can do, or dream you can, begin it. Boldness has genius, power and magic in it. —W. H. Murray, *Scottish Himalayan Expedition*

MOMENTUM IS THE SINGLE most important tool in your toolbox, and it's more than just about movement. You may come out of the starting gate with guns blazing, but then the fear parts show up, and you get stuck. Momentum is about creating a shift in your thinking. It's the experience you get when you're moving forward in your life, when you have a sense of progress. It's all the things that give your life oomph. Momentum needs space to grow. So look around and notice where you can start building momentum by creating more physical space around you, like in your office or your kitchen. When was the last time you spent a few hours decluttering anything? This doesn't have to be a big deal. Just start with one drawer or your clothes closet. Do a little at a time and keep going. You need space to breathe, to think, to contemplate new strategies, and to build momentum.

Start moving in your life in a different way. Mix it up a bit. If you always sleep in, get up an hour early. If you always go for a run in the morning, try walking around the track for a change. If you always eat eggs for breakfast, try a protein shake or toast and fruit. You're inviting your brain and body to open and be present in the world in new and different ways.

Momentum doesn't survive in a chaotic climate. It thrives on ease. What are some of the ways you can create more ease in your life? Staying away from the mall on a Saturday morning? Putting off the yard work for one more day to play tennis with your neighbor? Remember, momentum flows in easiness. Think of ways you can learn to be more available to people, to love a little better. Stop what you're doing for a moment and really listen to your son describing the argument he had with a friend today at school. Random acts of kindness do make a difference. They don't have to be big things.

Dig deep. Create the results you want for yourself in your mind first. See, feel, and experience the results you're committed to in your mind. Feel them in your body. Own them. Visualize them over and over.

Be specific about *what* you really want for yourself and *why*. Also, remember to look around and acknowledge the luck or grace that's already in your life right now.

Once you're clear on why you want what you want, begin building oomph. Simply understanding this stuff is the booby prize. You need to translate your goals into action. If you link enough pleasure to mastering something, you will. Engagement is everything. When you get excited enough, you'll get moving.

Keep visualizing what you want until it's second nature, and you don't have to think about it. Mastery is about accomplishment. Progress is a great motivator. *I'm sick of this* is a good place to start, and it's a common response I would expect to hear when I speak to groups and ask them why they want to make changes. Get yourself into a passionate place. Without passion, there's no energy.

Start with smaller and manageable markers along the way, like changing the time of your coffee break or altering your carpooling schedule. The small wins are your progress points. They keep you moving forward and on track. Do the little things well. Progress equals growth, and growth equals aliveness.

What does success look like for you? How do you want to spend your time? Think about what's really important to you and write your goals down. Put this list somewhere where you can easily see and review it.

Are the goals you describe really useful to you? Are they worth the effort it's going to take to pull them off? Are they a priority? Are there things you need to add or subtract from the list? There's power in clarity and commitment.

A study conducted among Harvard graduating students looked at how many of them had solid goals around how much money they wanted to make. Only 3% of the students had written their goals down. Ten years later, the same 3% who wrote their goals down were making more than the other 97% combined.

The problem is not always the problem. Sometimes the problem is whatever is blocking the problem's solution. Sometimes that's you. What steps do you need to take to squash what stops you? You don't have to be broken or broke in life.

Remembering that you are going to die is the best way I know to avoid the trap of thinking you have something to lose. —Steve Jobs, Co-founder, Apple

Chapter 9

Nowhere To Go But On

Without leaps of imagination or dreaming, we lose the excitement of possibilities. Dreaming, after all, is a form of planning. —Gloria Steinem

Wanting something is not enough. You must hunger for it. Your motivation must be absolutely compelling in order to overcome the obstacles that will invariably come your way. —Les Brown, American motivational speaker

GET CLEAR ON YOUR commitment to yourself. It's part of your hero's journey. Decide to *up the stakes*.

Why is change important to you? The plan is not the hard part. You can always come up with a plan. First, you decide why change is important to you. If you're clear on the answer to this, it'll give you the motivation you need to press through when things seem impossible. I would share with groups that getting clear on your *why* is the most important part of the process.

Trying on new behaviors when you feel fearful and uncertain is hard. Fear is what you deal with first before you start on the needed skills, because fear is in the way. How many people do you know who understand exactly what they need to do, but they never do it? Anyone can experiment, but once you make a commitment, it's hard for fear to stop you. You're overwriting old thought patterns here. You're becoming emotionally and mentally fit. It's going to feel awkward and scary at first.

Action is everything. When you try new behaviors and they don't work, you adjust and do something else. That's the plan in a nutshell. You just keep adjusting until you find what works. You're redesigning your life from the ground up, and it's going to look the way it looks.

In 1869, engineer John Roebling came up with a plan to build the Brooklyn Bridge. The suspension bridge spanned the East River from Brooklyn to Manhattan in New York City. Experts told him there was no way it could be done. The architect worked with his son, Washington, who was also an engineer, to design a plan to prove everyone wrong. The project was underway only a few months when Roebling was killed in an onsite accident. His son was badly hurt. Everyone thought the project would get scrapped because Roebling and his son were the only ones who knew how to pull it off.

Even though Washington was unable to move or talk, his mind was sharp. He developed a communication code with one finger. He tapped out instructions to engineers for thirteen years until the Brooklyn Bridge was completed in 1883. The bridge opened with a massive celebration.

Humans have been surviving and thriving hardship since the beginning. After the initial shock of grief wears off, many people realize the best way to honor their loved ones, if they passed, is not in perpetual upset, but by moving on and living the best life they can.

Some of the early research in the field reveals a series of predictable stages of grief, as in the teachings of Elisabeth Kübler-Ross. Not so, says George Bonanno, Professor of Clinical Psychology at Columbia University's Teachers College. There are no predictable stages.

Traditional grieving theories also speak of breaking the emotional ties with the deceased as a goal for moving on. Yet, the research shows grieving is more complex than that. Many healthy people still feel deeply connected to their loved ones long after they're gone. The research asserts that maintaining the emotional bond is actually healthy. Experiencing the continued presence of the deceased person soon after death might make you feel worse. But the same experience later on in the grieving process can be comforting.

Culture plays a big part too. In the West, we tend to be

science-minded and scoff at the thought of communicating with the dead. We're uncomfortable with such topics. Other cultures like China view communicating with the dead as a natural part of living and dying, and they practice rituals to honor the deceased in this way.

The Dahomey people of Western Africa have maintained many of their ancient ways. They celebrate the life of the deceased, but don't let things get too serious. They celebrate death by drinking, dancing, and singing that goes on all night. Their lightness helps relieve their grief, but that's not the only purpose. The primary purpose is to *amuse the dead*. According to their traditions, *to moralize to a dead person is both indelicate and senseless.* Their lighthearted approach to death often includes carnival-like elements and parades with costumed villagers.

The Mexican Day of the Dead (el Día de los Muertos) is another example of a culture with a different take on honoring death. In their tradition, families welcome back the souls of their deceased relatives for a brief reunion that includes celebration. Their annual rite features skeletons, altars, costumes and parades. The custom looks somewhat like our American Halloween. It's not. It's their lighthearted take on death, not unlike the Dahomey people. On this day, they believe the border between the spirit world and the real-world dissolves. The souls of the dead awaken and return to the living world to feast, drink, dance, and play music with their loved ones.

The Mexican is familiar with death, jokes about it, caresses it, sleeps with it, celebrates it; it is one of his favorite toys and his most steadfast love, said Octavio Paz, Mexican poet.

The latest research suggests that grief can actually deepen our connections, not only to those who remain alive but also to those who've passed on. It can generate a new sense of meaning in life, an innate resilience, a resilience that often doesn't require mental health professionals to overcome.

There is something wonderfully bold and liberating about saying yes to our entire imperfect and messy life. —Tara Brach, American Buddhist teacher

Chapter 10

Choose Gratitude

If the only prayer you ever say in your entire life is thank you, it will be enough.
—Meister Eckhart

It takes strength to make your way through grief, to grab hold of life, and let it pull you forward. —Patti Davis, American actress

GRIEF, LOSS, AND BETRAYAL can tenderize you and soften the hardness around your heart. If you love, you'll grieve. It's a given. And it's okay not to be okay about it. You're letting go of how things are supposed to look.

In a moment, we can shift our identity and step out of what's called the body of fear. We can release what we've carried when we were, as we can be, so loyal to our suffering, and become something bigger. —Jack Kornfield, American Buddhist teacher

Gratitude teaches that you can be thankful even when things look messy and when they feel awful. Challenge gloominess in your life. How loyal are you right now to your suffering, to your story? What, if anything, sustains you during times like this? Think about it.

Everyone gets stuck sometimes. Beware of learned helplessness. It's a state that happens after you've experienced a traumatic situation repeatedly. You come to believe that you can't control or change the situation, so you don't try even when opportunities for change become available. To overcome learned helplessness, focus on things you can control rather than what you can't. Learned optimism helps you to develop a more optimistic perspective when things look bleak. Once again, it's a shift in attitude. Without gratitude, there's no joy.

Everything is controlled by emotions. Are problems always your primary focus? What's your emotional home right now, anger, despair, grief? Where do you focus most, the past, present, or future? What are the two most stressful thoughts you think most often? The meaning you give something creates the emotion, and you have patterns of emotion.

If you don't have people in your life right now that you can talk to, then it's time to create a connection with someone—or a group of people—with whom you can be *real* with. When things fall apart, you'll need them. You also need something to look forward to at the end of your day; these people, animals and events will connect you back to what really matters to you. Use them. These are the people, animals, and events you want to lean into when things get tough.

Make up your mind to live in joy for just one day, even though you have all the facts. See what happens. People who have a sense of love and belonging in the world believe they're worthy of love and belonging. What if you're worthy already?

Gratitude turns what we have into enough, and more. It turns denial into acceptance, chaos into order, confusion into clarity ... it makes sense of our past, brings peace for today, and creates a vision for tomorrow.
—Melody Beattie, American author

Find gratitude for the simple things you sometimes take for granted. Be thankful for the hot shower that coaxed you awake this morning, the warm vegetable soup on your lunch table, the friend who remembered your birthday, the dog or cat who's always happy to see you come through the door. These are the things that make a life.

How about gratitude for your willingness and openness to rise up around your grief or betrayal and to continue on with life in a wholehearted way? That's real courage! You're moving from the known to the unknown, where all transformation happens. It feels yucky sometimes, but without these moments, there's no real growth.

You didn't think you could get through this, and yet, you're watching yourself get through this. That's progress. Maybe you're clumsy and have teary eyes some days; you're at a loss for what to say and do, but you show up anyway doing the next right thing, doing whatever comes next. Can you really expect more from yourself than that? You're enough!

Something as simple as a gratitude journal can make a big difference. Start by writing down three things a day you're grateful for. Studies show that people who practice gratitude experience more positive emotions, feel more alive, sleep better, express more compassion and kindness, and have stronger immune systems.

Gratitude leaves you in a place of humility. If you're grateful, you can't be angry and fearful too. When you count your blessings, the world changes. Gratitude is about faith in life. If you're short on faith in life, just be willing to be willing to be grateful. That's enough of a start for now. As gratitude grows, you'll get joyful for yourself and for other people. There's no greater gift than being grateful for the life you've been given, and gratitude leads to generosity. It's the fountain from which everything flows. Gratitude unlocks the best in life.

Your heart knows the answer. Your whole life exists in this moment, in this living moment. All points of power are right here. All the space and opportunity you need is right here. In a state of gratitude, you're saying yes to life. It's all you have, and it's enough!

———

In the end, though, maybe we must all give up trying to pay back the people in this world who sustain our lives. In the end, maybe it's wiser to surrender before the miraculous scope of human generosity and to just keep saying thank you, forever and sincerely, for as long as we have voices.

—Elizabeth Gilbert, American writer

Chapter 11

You Get What You Give

Any time you have an opportunity to make a difference in this world and you don't, then you are wasting your time on Earth. —Roberto Clemente

You cannot continue to succeed in the world or have a fulfilling life in the world unless you choose to use your life in the service somehow to others, and give back what you have been given. That's how you keep it. That's how you get it. That's how you grow it. —Oprah Winfrey, American talk show host

NONE of us got here without wounds. You have a story, but you're *not* your story. When all is said and done, you'll get what you give in life, and the giving you do doesn't have to be extravagant.

You're wired to give, to spread kindness in small ways. You grow because you can give—sometimes it's as simple as a heartfelt thank you to the waitress who's probably working for little money and may have a sick baby at home. Maybe it's helping your neighbor find her dog. It all counts. Be a student of your life, instead of an expert. Try smiling more.

When you find yourself stressed out, stop and think of three things you're grateful for and then see what happens! You're learning new ways of paying attention. Trust me. You're building an unshakable foundation.

Your egoic operating system wants to make life all about you all the time. It wants to make everything go your way and look exactly how you said it should look. When it doesn't turn out, you get upset. Life simply isn't that way. In my talks, I would speak to the strategies that remind people to take their attention off themselves for a bit, and see what they can do for someone else. It can be an instant cure-all.

At the end, it's not about what you have, or even what you've accomplished. It's about who you lifted up, who you've made better. It's about what you've given back. —Denzel Washington, American actor

A young woman moved to California on her own with her dog. Shortly after arriving, she was involved in a serious car accident. The dog was with her. There was no one for her to call for help in the emergency. The paramedics and firefighters who showed up on the scene not only saved her life, they took her dog back to the fire station and kept him entertained while she was recuperating in the hospital.

When the nurses heard she had no one to come get her, no way to get home, and had lost most of her belongings in the car crash, they raised hundreds of dollars of their own money to get her home and to help her rebuild. Everyone benefits when you're kind and generous, no matter how big or small. You know that!

Although the world is full of suffering, it is full also of the overcoming of it. –Helen Keller, American author

It feels good when you do something good for someone else. Doesn't it? Studies reveal that any selfless act you do for others is connected to positive physical and mental outcomes for you and them. Research at the Cleveland Clinic reveals that this includes lower blood pressure, increased self-esteem, less incidence of depression, lower stress levels, and even longer life and more happiness.

Giving back means different things to different people. Decide for yourself what it means to you. It could be donating time to a non-profit you value. It could be giving money. It could be hanging out with a friend in hospice who has few visitors.

When you help others who have less, giving so they can have enough, it reminds you to be grateful for what you have. It also builds relationships with the people you're serving. You get to be part of something bigger than just you and your little world.

Yep, you're here to serve. It gives your life purpose and meaning. Especially as you age, a sense of purpose makes life worth living. It makes life meaningful. What causes are important to you? What experiences do you have that could benefit someone else? Think about giving back more.

Change happens when people join in common goals. You become part of a momentum that shifts things. It's an opportunity to make a difference. Results feel good. By being part of a team and working on an issue that's important to you, you feel good.

Jane Goodall is former president of Advocates for Animals, an organization that campaigns against the use of animals in medical research, zoos, farming, and sport.

With only a notebook and a pair of binoculars, Jane went to Tanzania at age 26 to study wild chimpanzees. She won the trust of these shy beings and her research revealed that chimpanzees form complex social bonds, make and use tools, hunt and eat meat, and display emotions like humans. Her work transformed the misconceptions about the lives of these primates. It led Jane to be an animal rights advocate.

Jane credits her parents with encouraging her curiosity about animals. She tells the story of how, as a toddler, she brought a handful of earthworms into her bedroom. Instead of being irritated or horrified, her mother simply urged Jane to return the creatures to the soil outside, where they could live and thrive. It was a simple lesson that had a profound impact on a young girl. By protecting chimpanzees and encouraging people to conserve the natural world we all share, Jane reminds us that everyone's life gets better.

You cannot get through a single day without having an impact on the world around you. What you do makes a difference, and you have to decide what kind of difference you want to make. —Jane Goodall

Chapter 12

Everything Comes And Goes

Every great dream begins with a dreamer. Always remember, you have within you the strength, the patience, and the passion to reach for the stars, to change the world. —Harriet Tubman

Personal transformation can and does have global effects. As we go, so goes the world, because the world is us. The revolution that will save the world is ultimately a personal one. —Marianne Williamson, American author

WE LIVE IN A WORLD of change. Awareness allows you to be present with the changes. These are the seasons of your life, and they include sorrow and joy, night and day, gain and loss, pleasure and pain. You can't have one without the other. It's just the way it is. Problems make you grow.

Sometimes the hard things you go through are the things that open your heart. That's just what it took! Who knows why? Maybe it's divine orchestration? Maybe what happened to you is actually a setup for what's coming, not a setback. It's that old adage about how are you viewing the glass, half-empty or half-full.

Hang out with people who are like-hearted. Turn up the volume on your innate wisdom, and turn down the volume on self-doubt. Self-doubt kills more dreams than anything else. There's a knowing in you that is bigger than who you think you are. Listen for that truth. Pay attention to your patterns, some of which probably don't serve you. Interrupt the patterns that don't work. Be open to redesigning your life, to setting new standards.

Challenges are inevitable. Letting go of the delusion that things won't change empowers the people I coach. You and the life you lead are constantly changing. Nothing is permanent. Nothing. Everything, including yourself, has an expiration date. Navigating all this with an open heart is your job, and some days it's sure a lot easier than others.

You're on reset. What you're experiencing right now is not the end of your story—unless you say so! Something else is going to show up; it always does. A well-lived life begins with you. Having an open heart and quiet mind softens your travels. You don't have to be a pinball. You can learn the things you need to know.

The grief and loss process takes time. Sometimes it demands that you find a place of rest in the middle of chaos. Sometimes it demands you simply allow the pain to be here. Slow down. Relax. Breathe. The *dark night of the soul* is your personal invitation to change.

Fear expressed allows for release, and conscious breathing brings you into your body. It doesn't matter *where* you start in your journey; it matters *that* you start. Be kind to yourself. Connect with your wise self. Clarity is power. As Rumi said, *Live life as if everything is rigged in your favor.*

Create certainty by imaging it. Most stress that you experience is in your mind. Be a force for good. Start your day with a sense of gratitude. You have work to do to move on, but you don't have to do it alone.

If you have emotional vampires in your life, you don't have to close your heart, but you also don't allow them to take you down. Emotional vampires don't feed on your blood, they feed on your energy. They sometimes show up as narcissists. They're easy to spot because their eyes glaze over when you begin to speak. They're endlessly needy, act like victims, lack real empathy, feel entitled, and they leave you feeling exhausted. Narcissists are adults who never grew up. Estimates suggest they're emotionally 8-10 years old, and will use up your time and life force if you let them. They're tornadoes ripping through your life. They smell vulnerability and prey on it. Don't feed the beast. This is where boundaries come into play. *No* is a complete sentence. Strong boundaries allow you to feel safe, heard, and respected. Sometimes the best way to handle these folks is to have no contact. Not everybody you lose is a loss.

Remember the mindfulness piece. Being mindful is about accepting these situations as they are, feeling your feelings, accepting the reality of change, and discovering ways to move on with your life. At the end of the day, that's all there is to do, and you never do it perfectly.

Be willing to take uncomfortable actions. They're leading you in the direction you want to go. Know that there will be times when the only appropriate action for you is to bear your troubles until a better day.

Remember meditation can be an enzyme for relief. If you can't sit still for long, think of it as quiet time. Just sit down and be quiet for twenty minutes. It's not about avoiding the unpleasant; it's about being aware, quieting the mind, and tending your heart. Get focused on what you want and go for it. Get clear on your reasons *why* first, the results will follow. Find people who are already living the life you want and model them. You need to witness someone who is already doing this, someone who's playing a bigger game than you. See yourself achieving your goals. Visualize this picture over and over. Reinforce what works and remember to pat yourself on the back. It's not enough to simply understand all of this. Take your understanding and turn it into action. You're rewiring your brain and it works.

In many ways, you're befriending your brokenness. You're inviting your brokenness to have a seat at the table with you, so you can hear what it has to say, learn from it, honor it, and grow. It got you here to this present moment where you now have the chance to choose a new way.

To me, going deep means questioning whatever holds me back from experiencing wisdom and love. —Trudy Goodman, American author

ONE LAST MESSAGE TO YOU!

Congratulations

None of this works if you don't take action. You *can* be brave and afraid at the same time. Honest. Invest in you. Connection is *why* you are here, and to really connect, you have to be vulnerable, to let yourself be seen. Change happens through self-acceptance, and you can be that loving and kind person to yourself as you step into your new way of doing life. Everything does change in life, but it also creates an opportunity for new beginnings.

Life is not fair, but problems are rarely permanent. Researchers say our brains are hardwired for negativity, and it's the negative things that grab your attention first. It's an evolutionary thing, the brain's attempt to protect you in threatening situations. It's like you're having a great day at work, then and one person says something rude to you. You spend the rest of the day ruminating about it. Are you making the situation worse? How do you act when you feel threatened? Breakdowns are inevitable. When you find yourself focusing only on the negative, look to reframe what happened in a different way. Understand your conditioning is at work. This doesn't mean closing your eyes to reality; it simply means refocusing, so you give equal weight to the good stuff too.

One of the most powerful skills you can develop is the ability to laugh when you get stressed and to find gratitude in moments of sadness. Joy is a decision. It starts when you let go of how life is supposed to be and start accepting life the way it actually is. You're stepping into unchartered territory. You're learning to be comfortable in your own skin. *Wherever you go, go with your whole heart,* Confucius said.

You'll get stuck sometimes. When you get stuck, just do one thing. Reach out. Make a call, write a letter, journal, or have an in-person conversation. Work with what's right in front of you. That'll get your energy moving again. I urge people I coach to have the courage to let themselves mess up. You never do it perfectly, anyway. The important point is you have the power to choose what you focus on. Stress doesn't come from facts. Stress comes from the meaning you give facts. When you craft a new meaning, you get a new life! Can you laugh while you fix your problems? Can you sidestep the melodrama?

Growing and giving, they are what life is about. Are you willing to learn to love better? Decide now that you're worthy of love and belonging, and that going forward, you're committed to loving with your whole heart even though there are no guarantees. Let yourself be seen. A fearless, compassionate attitude toward your pain is everything. Self-care is where healing begins. Believe you can create a new future and you will!

Jump, and you will find out how to unfold your wings as you fall, said Ray Bradbury, American author.

ACKNOWLEDGMENTS

Over the years, many people have shared books, ideas, mentoring, and love that has inspired my life, each in a different way. It's impossible to thank everyone, and I apologize for anyone not listed. Please know, I appreciate the contribution you are to my life.

Jordan O'Connor McKittrick, Tony Robbins, Brené Brown, Anne Lamott, James Malinchak, Nick and Megan Unsworth, Dean Graziosi, Jack Kornfield, Maria Shriver, Sharon Salzberg, Michael Singer, Ram Dass, Isabel Lopez, Scott Allan, Maya Angelou, Viola Davis, Pema Chödrön, Steve Jobs, Danna Faulds, Trudy Goodman, Sarah Gingell, Mary Oliver, Tara Brach, Les Brown, Oprah Winfrey, Natalie Goldberg, Patti Davis, Melody Beattie, Marianne Williamson, Jamie Anderson, Zoe Kravitz, The Beatles, Rumi, Joan Halifax, Gloria Steinem, Doug Cooper, Denzel Washington, Tim and Wendy Taylor, Helen Keller, Neale Donald Walsh, Kim McMillen, Jane Goodall, Elizabeth Gilbert, Octavio Paz, Harriet Tubman, Terry afnd Susan O'Connor, Don and Mary Ellen O'Connor, Kathleen Steppling, Paige and Rick Van Sickle, Joan Plummer, Julie and Brian Downey, Leda and Jack Mance, Jackie Rahm, Alice O'Connor, Uma Markus, Bob and Judy Schmader, Star, Lawrence and Irene Cook, Gary McGraime, Frank Ostaseski, Barbara Kazen, Jud Little, Tashai Lovington, Al-Anon, Alcoholics

Anonymous, ACA, Elisabeth Kübler-Ross, Norman Vincent Peale, W.H. Murray, C.S. Lewis, Ray Bradbury.

A Free BONUS RESOURCE for you
www.FreeGiftFromRosemary.com

One in-depth training video on
keeping your heart open through grief and betrayal

ABOUT ROSEMARY

Rosemary O'Connor McKittrick, MA, is a writer, storyteller, speaker and consultant focusing on people who are Aging with Heart. She offers tools that empower people to live more fully, no matter how old they are. Spoken from the heart, her book is a return to basics around weathering the inevitable grief we all face.

Rosemary is committed to supporting individuals in living their best life by filling the gap between where they are now and where they want to be. Her holistic approach brings clarity, direction, and support to clients. Are you spinning? Feeling stuck? Working with Rosemary, you'll discover new possibilities to get you back on track. Bigger goals. Bigger actions. Bigger results. Contact Rosemary today for consulting, coaching, or to speak to your group. Get clear on the next steps in your journey.

Life begins at the end of your comfort zone. —Neale Donald Walsch, American author

Rosemary O'Connor McKittrick
40 Calle Debra
Santa Fe, NM 87507
505-690-1841
RosemaryMcKittrick@comcast.net